What to Expect When Starting Krav Maga

A Krav Maga Journey™ Guide

Second Edition

Krav Maga Journey

An average guy's journey through the world of Krav Maga

Copyright © 2014 by Craig A. De Ruisseau and Krav Maga Journey. All rights reserved. No part of this publication may be used without the author's written consent. Any printout of this publication is solely for the use of the purchaser and is not to be loaned, copied, or distributed in any form.

ISBN: 9781500544553

Cover Design by Craig A. De Ruisseau

Produced in the United States of America

Dedicated to Helen, Jocelyn, and Evan

DISCLAIMER	6
WHO AM I?	7
WHAT IS KRAV MAGA?	10
What Krav Maga Is	10
What Krav Maga Isn't	11
Is Krav Maga for Everyone?	12
FEAR	13
Feeling Fear	13
Moving Beyond Fear	14
CLASS STRUCTURE	16
Warm-up	16
Drills	17
Sparring	17
Conditioning	18
Shoes	18
SOME WORDS OF ENCOURAGEMENT	20
THE TIPS	22
Tip #1: Stay open-minded	22
Tip #2: Don't bring in baggage	24
Tip #3: Be receptive to other people	25
Tip #4: You will get hurt	25
Tip #5: Don't get frustrated	27
Tip #6: Don't compare your performance or endurance to others	28
Tip #7: Continue exercise outside of class	28
Tip #8: It will be tougher than any other physical regimen you've experienced	29
Tip #9: This is Reality Based Self-Defense, not an aerobics class	30
Tip #10: Sparring is essential so embrace it	30
Tip #11: It never *ever* gets easier	38
Tip #12: True motivation comes from within	38
Tip #13: Favor speed and aggression over power and technique	39
Tip #14: There will be casualties	40
Tip #15: You MUST drink plenty of fluids	40
Tip #16: Later on, you'll see that even lower belts have something to teach	41
Tip #17: Use your belt as a goal but don't obsess about it	42
Tip #18: Buy equipment right the first time	43

TIP #19: BE GRACIOUS	44
TIP #20: DON'T TALK SMACK ABOUT PEOPLE	44
TIP #21: YOU WILL LOSE WEIGHT BUT ONLY IF YOU MAKE IT A LIFESTYLE COMMITMENT	45
TIP #22: THERE WILL ALWAYS BE SOMEONE BETTER THAN YOU	46
TIP #23: IT TAKES A LOT OF COMMITMENT	46
TIP #24: NEVER LET YOUR 'GOOD' BE YOUR 'BEST'	47
TIP #26: THIS ISN'T AN ACTION MOVIE WITH YOU IN THE STARRING ROLE	48
TIP #27: YOU ARE STRONGER THAN YOU THINK	49
TIP #28: YOU WILL ONLY GET OUT OF IT WHAT YOU PUT INTO IT	49
TIP #29: IT'S NEVER TOO SOON TO WEAR YOUR CUP	50
TIP #30: EAT BEFORE CLASS TO FUEL YOUR WORKOUT	51
TIP #31: CUT YOUR NAILS	52
TIP #32: ADOPT A HABIT OF BEING METICULOUSLY CLEAN	52
TIP #33: IF YOU GET CUT, BANDAGE IT UP	55
TIP #34: IF YOU USE COMMUNITY EQUIPMENT, WIPE IT DOWN WHEN YOU'RE DONE	55
TIP #35: HANG OUT A LITTLE AFTER CLASS	56
TIP #36: TEMPER YOUR REALITY-BASED SELF-DEFENSE WITH SOME REALITY	57
TIP #37: FOCUS ON WHAT YOU'RE DOING WELL INSTEAD OF WHAT YOU'RE DOING POORLY	58
TIP #38: YOU'VE GOT TO UPGRADE AND DOWNSIZE YOUR BODY	59
TIP #39: BE WILLING TO ACCEPT CRITIQUES AND FEEDBACK	59
TIP #40: LEAVE YOUR EGO AT THE DOOR	61
TIP #41: CHOOSE PARTNERS WISELY AND MIX IT UP	62
TIP #42: HAVE FUN!	65
YOUR TURN	**66**
CHEAT SHEET	**67**
ABOUT THE AUTHOR	**69**

Disclaimer

Krav Maga is an intense martial art involving many techniques, drills, and exercises that will challenge your body and mind in ways that you likely have never experienced. It is for this reason that you should carefully and honestly assess your body's abilities and limits so that you might train as safely as possible.

As with all exercise regimens, it is suggested that you consult with your doctor prior to undertaking Krav Maga training to ensure that you are cleared for the rigors that lay ahead of you. This is of particular importance if you are overweight, asthmatic, or have any chronic injuries, particularly to the back, knees, shoulders, or neck.

Who Am I?

Before we get off to the races, I'd like to pause a minute to get you situated with who's writing this Guide. In other words, why should you take it seriously?

I'm an American male born in New England. I began my training in Krav Maga back in June 2011 when I was 42 years old. At the time, I was hardly in peak physical condition; I was 6' 4" and 315 pounds. You don't need a BMI calculator to know that I was overweight. If you are in a similar situation with your body, I'm here to tell you that there is hope if you're willing to commit.

I wanted to put together a blog after researching various martial arts and being drawn to Krav Maga. I was a little frustrated by the lack of information on the web about the style, particularly information about what the style involved from a training standpoint. Sure, you can find videos of master practitioners demonstrating techniques on willing students and seemingly endless clips from videos for sale but there was a definite gap there that I thought I could help fill. Even if no one visited the blog I felt that it would serve as a cathartic diary for me, tracing my steps along the path to earning my Black Belt.

I am not an extreme athlete nor am I breezing through the ranks. I struggle just like everyone else; sometimes it feels like I do more than others. I am not a member of an elite military Special Forces unit who yawns through drills and rolls his eyes during sparring. I started when I was a middle-aged guy looking to attain a higher fitness level, regain my sense of dedication and confidence, get off many of my medications, learn some valuable self-defense skills, and meet some new people with similar goals.

What you will read in this Guide is something I wish I had when I started out. So much was unknown to me at the time. I had so many questions and no one was available to answer them reliably. I knew next to nothing about Krav Maga, other than what I saw on an episode of *Human Weapon* on *The History Channel* or gleaned from the Internet. I knew nothing of what to expect or what kind of attitude I should be bringing. I would have been so much better prepared if I had this kind of Guide available, which is why I decided to put one together.

Some people wonder at this Guide's diminutive size. Why is it on the small side of things? Surely there's a lot to know before starting Krav Maga – why isn't this book bigger? There's actually a good reason. This book is intended to be a quick read, something a new student on the cusp of taking their first class can go through in one or two sittings. It's designed to be "just in time" knowledge that you can absorb right before starting to give you just what you need right here, right now. If a book like this were to be one that was completely exhaustive, was composed of many hundreds of pages, and took the typical reader weeks to get through, it would hardly be much use to a student whose first class is the day after tomorrow.

It is my sincere hope that you find the information in here valuable and worth your time. I want to make your experience less stressful and give you some tools that will help you get the most out of it in a shorter time than it took me.

By looking into Krav Maga, getting your hands on this Guide, and thinking seriously about what it all means, you have taken your first big step. This isn't easy and I know because I've been there too.

I wish you luck, better health, success, and profound happiness in your personal journey on the road to excellence.

Craig De Ruisseau
August 3, 2014

What is Krav Maga?

Krav Maga is shrouded in a lot of hype and burdened by many misconceptions. It has been sensationalized to an extent as it can be seen in many Hollywood movies and seems to be the go-to martial art these days when directors want to get their characters kicking some bad guy's butt. *Taken*, *Enough*, *Cross*, *Mission: Impossible* and *Blood Diamond* are just a few. I hear the actor Daniel Craig also trained to make his James Bond more of a tough guy.

What Krav Maga Is

Krav Maga is "real world" self-defense, in the category of *Reality-Based Self-Defense* (RBSD) martial arts. Unlike many traditional martial arts, there are no competitions, no tournaments, and no trophies. Not that there's anything wrong with any of those, mind you. Some Krav Maga schools don't use belts though, contrary to popular belief, belts were in fact used by Krav Maga's founder.

Krav Maga is a martial art whose origins are rooted in the war-torn country of Israel. The name loosely translates into "contact combat" and was developed initially for the Israeli military in the 1940's by a Slovakian-Israeli man named Imi Lichtenfeld. Mr. Lichtenfeld, with a background in Judo, wrestling, and boxing, created the martial art using his extensive fighting knowledge, first-hand experience, and his uncanny knack for developing effective self-defense techniques. Krav Maga teaches not only empty-handed combat maneuvers but also defensive techniques against guns, knives, baseball bats, and other weapons.

Krav Maga was refined in the 1950's as Mr. Lichtenfeld tested and tuned the martial art in the trenches of warfare, ensuring that the style would not suffer from being *theoretical* martial arts but rather would employ *practical*, real world techniques proven to be effective. In the mid 1960's, Krav Maga began to also become available to law enforcement agencies and also, in a somewhat adapted form, to civilians. It's designed to help keep you safe. The motto of Krav Maga is: "So that one may walk in peace".

Mr. Lichtenfeld died in 1998 leaving behind a legacy and students who have evangelized Krav Maga tirelessly across the globe. The martial art has become one of the most popular martial arts styles, practiced by many thousands of students worldwide.

What Krav Maga Isn't

As great as Krav Maga is, it is not some magical form of self-defense that will turn its practitioners into super-human, indestructible warriors. Marketing is meant to sell products and services pure and simple. In many schools that offer Krav Maga, the expectations and promised results of training just a few months are pushed beyond reality into fantasy-land. Yes, Krav Maga is very effective. Yes, it gets people in shape. Yes, it can potentially save your life someday. But is it something that will protect you from every threat in every situation against every attacker out there? Think again. No such style exists. Despite Krav Maga's greatness it is always up to the practitioner using it, the circumstances they are under, and sometimes the luck of the draw that will determine the outcome of a particular encounter.

I wholeheartedly endorse Krav Maga to everyone looking to protect themselves and their loved ones. But you need to go in with eyes wide open and with realistic expectations about Krav Maga and what it can do for you.

Is Krav Maga for Everyone?

Although the fundamental techniques of Krav Maga can be performed by practically anyone, the martial art is not for everybody any more than square dancing, fire-eating, or foie gras is. Like all martial arts, Krav Maga has a high dropout rate among new students, as much due to it being a physically demanding nature as it is people realizing that it is simply not for them.

Nevertheless, if you decide that Krav Maga is right for you, and you're willing to commit to it, you will succeed regardless of age, gender, or physical fitness level. I started my Krav Maga journey in my 40's, obese and incapable of walking up a flight of stairs without getting winded. Now, several years later, I am in the best shape of my life. I've lost all of my excess weight, my confidence is higher, and I now enjoy several strenuous classes a week.

Fear

"I must not fear.
Fear is the mind-killer.
Fear is the little-death that brings total obliteration.
I will face my fear.
I will permit it to pass over me and through me.
And when it has gone past I will turn the inner eye to see its path.
Where the fear has gone there will be nothing.
Only I will remain."
~ Dune (Frank Herbert)

Feeling Fear

Let's be real and start right here. Unless you're wired differently than everyone else, you are nervous and scared nearly out of your mind. After all, you're starting out in a new place with new people doing something you've never done before. Most of us feel nervous taking a new bus for the first time and you're starting Krav Maga, a violent form of self-defense used by the Israeli military and law enforcement agencies around the globe. A style that's renowned for its brutality and effectiveness in putting the smack-down on people. Yes, being scared is pretty much a given.

Unfortunately, you're going to feel the fear; there's no getting around it completely. But hopefully this Guide will put your mind at ease a little and the small fee you paid for it will be worth it many times over.

I remember one of my first moments so well. It was going to be my introductory session at 6:30 p.m. and I was sitting with my sweaty hands on the wheel of my parked car, the school looming large through the car's windshield. I was nervous and had no clue what to expect. I was very overweight and in pretty lousy shape. I didn't know who my intro session was with or what kind of vibes I'd get from them or the school. Was this like Cobra Kai, the teacher like John Kreese (I'm referencing the original Karate Kid movie here)? I felt fear. I felt it strongly. I had flickers of doubt in my head and I'm pretty sure you do right about now too.

I thought: "What am I doing here?", "I'm 42 years old for cryin' out loud – am I nuts?", "Is it too late to back out?" Nevertheless, I swallowed hard, screwed up my courage...and walked in that door.

Moving Beyond Fear

Turns out it wasn't so bad after all. You can read about it more in the "First Lesson, Deconstructed" post on my blog (kravmagajourney.com) where I go into more detail about what went down and how I did. Suffice it to say here that it was physically and emotionally rough, not to mention hotter than the hinges of Hell, but I made it out alive.

Fast forward slightly. The intro was now out of the way and I was going into the dojo with people who were all more experienced than me by the very fact that it was my first minute in a full class. Even though the intro went well the anxiety was back in the red again. I was starting over back in unknown territory.

That day changed my life. I don't mean that as hyperbole. I mean that it literally changed my life. Don't believe me? Here's a sampling of what I've gained by conquering my fear and starting:

- I'm more fit than I've ever been in my life
- I've lost more weight than I ever thought possible
- I'm off my high blood pressure medication

In addition to these, I've met dozens of top-notch people and made many friends for life, gained invaluable confidence in myself and my ability to take on challenges, learned how to protect myself and my loved ones, and have learned how to set and meet tough personal goals.

If you are anything like me then you are about to undertake an experience like you've never had before, and it will change you for the better in nearly every aspect of your life.

Take a deep breath and jump in.

"Fear is met and destroyed with courage."
~James F. Bell

Class Structure

There are hundreds if not *thousands* of schools and several organizations that offer Krav Maga around the globe. As such, there is really no single class format, shared by all as the de facto standard. That said, it's possible to lay out some universal components so that you can at least get an *idea* what class might be like at a school you are considering. For a more definitive idea you obviously would want to drop by your school, talk with the teachers and students, and see if they offer a trial program to allow you to experience a class first-hand.

Warm-up

We all know that you can't jump into class and start going *bananas* without a good warm-up – at least not without risking pulls, strains, and other sorts of painful consequences. Classes often start with a light jog and jumping jacks, transitioning into sprints and other similar routines. The options are obviously endless and vary not only by school but by instructor. The end goal of these warm-ups, however, is the same: to get the blood flowing and start warming up those muscles and tendons.

There are other varieties of warm-ups that sometimes get brought into play to warm up the upper body. These can include pushups, shadow boxing, partner 'shoulder touch' drills, etc. Good schools keep it mixed and interesting so things never get boring for students.

Drills

There are lesson plans that schools follow, varying from place to place, but regardless of the school and curriculum, once the technique is taught it's time to put it into practice. Drills are the way that schools bring pairs of students, or small or large groups, to apply the lessons in a realistic setting. Realistic as in, high adrenaline and lots of physical contact.

To get the most out of these, you have to dive in and get involved. Some people can never get the mindset to "click" and go through drills as a series of moves that they're parroting. Other, more successful students embrace the lesson and throw themselves into each and every drill like their life depends on it. Someday it just might.

Sparring

Sparring is one of those things that everyone is terrified to do at first. Many people never quite shake that feeling either. They enter the dojo every time sparring's on the agenda with a lump in their throat and quaking in their boots.

Sparring, however, is essential to the proper development of your self-defense. Even if you are like most, that is, not training to be a professional fighter, you will get profound benefits from sparring. Learning to manage your fear, understanding your ranges, toughening your body, and building fight endurance are a few of the many benefits that sparring will provide to you.

Conditioning

All the techniques in the world aren't worth a hill of beans without a conditioned body. If you have little strength and endurance, Krav Maga is worthless. You can watch countless videos about Krav Maga, read endless books on technique, and even sit on the sidelines of a class for months on end, but without getting in the game and bringing your body to a point where it needs to be physically, it is pretty much worthless. Your body is your instrument for self-defense and needs to be as developed as much it can be, regardless of age or excuses.

Conditioning exercise options are endless but the one thing they have in common is that they're designed to not only build up your body's strength, flexibility, and endurance but to get your body into a state of near exhaustion so that you can train in a situation that mimics what your body will be like in a real-life attack. That is, the deadened feeling throughout your whole body that is similar to the body's sensation following the adrenaline dump that occurs following the traumatic experience of being in a street fight.

Shoes

Though not universal, many Krav Maga schools mandate that their students train in shoes. The shoes are often wrestling shoes but it's not uncommon for people to also wear MMA-type shoes or even running shoes, provided that the shoes are used exclusively in the dojo and not on the street. This keeps the mats free of outside gunk like gum, dirt, and dog poop. Other schools, mine included, have their students train barefoot most of the time, though you have the option to wear indoor-only shoes if you'd like.

I go back and forth myself. This is especially true if I'm nursing a toe injury. Shoes give your feet that added protection while your toes are on the mend.

No one can say which is better. It's more of a personal or school preference. One could argue that the odds of being attacked while barefoot are slim (unless it's at a beach perhaps) so you're better off using shoes. Others swear by the added durability of a fighter who has the toughened feet of a barefoot-trained martial artist.

I say follow school protocol first, your personal preference second. Both work well but only one will work better for you and it's your job to find out which one that is.

Some Words of Encouragement

You are about to embark on your own journey and, the way I see it, you're in one of two camps: you're either going to be one of the great majority of people who tries it and drops out or one of the minority who commits to the long, painful, arduous journey. I hope you join us in the second group. There is no finish line, only milestones along the way to mark our progress.

For me, there were a few points along the way, particularly early on in my training, when I wondered if I was cut out for it. As I said earlier, I began my personal journey overweight, out of shape, and prone to getting winded walking up a flight of stairs.

Those first few months were pretty rough. I had almost constant "runner's knee" (*patellar tendinitis* or "jumper's knee") from the impact of jumping a lot during warm-ups, was sore every day, was drenched in sweat within minutes of starting class, and developed some minor injury or another every week. I'm pretty sure my wife and friends thought I was nuts but a couple years later, here I am – far slimmer, in the best shape of my life, and with a quiet confidence developed from countless grueling classes and drills.

Regardless of where you are starting, if you have the dedication and want it badly enough you will succeed. It's that simple. If you are overweight, older, short, tall, asthmatic...whatever. If you have the iron determination to make it, you will make it. There are no exceptions.

Think about that for a minute and let it sink in. If you commit to it and do your best, never quit, and live the lifestyle, you will succeed. That is a relief when you think about it.

Now, for everyone, this is a real tall order. I see a lot of White Belts join our school and the vast majority don't appear to be all that athletic. I've seen some of these same people rise to the challenge and become extremely fit and profoundly effective in Krav Maga. It can and does happen all the time.

You can do this.

It requires the right mindset, patience, dedication, and the belief that you are capable. I'm living, breathing proof.

The Tips

Here's where we get into some solid ideas to help you get the most out of your training as you start out on your journey. How do I know they're solid? Well, because I've been there myself, because I have been around hundreds of people who have also been there, and because I've applied them and seen them work. These are the tips I wish I had when I started and I now give them to you. My advice to you is that you review them before every class for the first few weeks so they sink in. If you follow the guidance in this Guide I can assure you that you will make the experience a whole lot easier and more fulfilling.

Tip #1: Stay open-minded

Unless you are in the rare situation of having a fellow student next to you who joined on the same day, *everyone* knows more than you in your first class. If you're anything like me that can be a pretty scary thought. You're the "new kid on the block", The Freshman, The Rookie, the one who knows the absolute least about Krav Maga in the entire dojo.

It's pretty daunting for everyone for different reasons. If the student is a teen, for example, they are likely self-conscious to begin with. For a male teenager, in particular, class can be a major strain on the ego. Males in today's society are often led to believe they're macho and capable of throwing a punch when things get bad. First-person shooter video games, the popularity of MMA and wrestling, ever-present violent movies, and surging testosterone coursing through their veins only add to boys' distorted, powerful, but most of the time delusional self-image of themselves. Now they are in a classroom of strangers with a big, obvious White Belt strapped around them, marking them as someone who knows "nothing". They might be a star quarterback but here they are a newbie. Some guys have problems with this abrupt change of status in the pecking order.

For adults, on the other hand, it can be tough for other reasons. After all, maybe they are very successful in a career where they have responsibilities for controlling millions of dollars, large teams of employees, maybe they even own an entire business themselves. It may have taken years to achieve the level of professional respect that they get from 9:00 - 5:00 at their job. Then they are in a classroom – taught in some cases by instructors half their age – and surrounded by many students who are *all* more advanced than them in Krav Maga. This can be a real blow to some adults' egos.

If the student is a female, regardless of age, it can be very intimidating too. It's a very physical environment and they are going to be hitting and being hit by men and other women. In general, women are not as violent or physical as men. Most women don't fantasize about fights, root for certain MMA contenders in cage matches, or get into bar fights. To make matters worse, in some classes they will also be rolling around on the floor with a sweaty classmate (male and female) and being seen in public a sweaty mess. Some females embrace this while some have a difficult time with it.

Regardless of your age, gender, income, or career achievements outside your school's four walls, you have to remember to be receptive to everything, accept that this might be different from anything you've tried before and embrace it, adopting a positive attitude from that point on. Don't let your ego get in the way. Don't think of students or instructors in terms of their age but rather in terms of their experience.

Tip #2: Don't bring in baggage

If you've learned from other styles let them go. Krav Maga is unlike most traditional martial arts styles and, although some of what you've learned elsewhere might help, in the beginning it will do nothing but trip you up. Try to leave that stuff at the door.

I myself came to the school with some minor experience in *Uechi-ryu* from about 25 years previous. I didn't get very far in that style due to me quitting a year or so after starting to go to college. That small amount of training as a teen stayed with me and when I started Krav Maga, I was under the mistaken notion that it would help me. I tried to quietly carry some of the ideas into class with me, whether they are stances or stretches or striking techniques. In the end, this did nothing but disrupt the learning for me and make me profoundly confused about footwork.

Don't get me wrong. I'm not saying that previous martial arts experience is useless and can't help. That's not true. In fact, for some it will probably be a great benefit – provided that you bring it in with the right mindset. If you accept it for what it is, "previous martial arts experience", then you will probably be okay. Some things may translate well or help make learning Krav Maga easier. On the other hand, some things you've learned in the past may make it harder because you are reluctant to let them go to learn something new.

In either case, make sure that you don't come in with an air of self-entitlement because of your prior training. I've seen some students come in with a kind of attitude like, "I'm a Black Belt in _____. I'm now giving Krav Maga a shot to see how poorly it compares. I doubt it can live up to how great _____ is!"

That sort of adversarial attitude won't get you far. If a former style is that near and dear to you, maybe you should consider continuing it. If you have tired of your former style and want to learn something new and different then release your baggage and come in fresh with an open mind. It will get you a lot farther.

Tip #3: Be receptive to other people

Don't go all *intense* on everyone and be only in it for yourself by ignoring everyone else and being stand-offish. It's tempting to adopt this kind of attitude if you are feeling overwhelmed with the newness of it all and if being junior is threatening your masculinity.

You need to mingle and get to know others, even if you are introverted and shy. This is a long journey and you'll need companions to come along with you to share in your triumphs and your failures. Trust me; it makes it much more fun and rewarding.

Tip #4: You will get hurt

Regardless of the safety precautions and no matter how safe you are, you will get hurt. If there is one thing I can tell you with the utmost certainty it is that you are going to incur injuries of all shapes and sizes. I'm not talking blood spurting from arteries and compound fractures of the leg. By and large, I am talking about very minor to moderate injuries. Sometimes it will just be a bruise or scratch here or there and sometimes it will be a little more serious like a strain, pull, or fracture.

This is part of the game and although you should be prepared for it, you shouldn't be scared.

I would say, on average, I get some sort of injury or another every week or two. It's unusual for me to be walking onto the mat without at least *something* bothering me to some degree or another. Few Krav Maga practitioners are 100% injury free all the time. I can tell you right now as you're reading this sentence that I probably got hurt last class. The kinds of injuries I've had include, but aren't limited to:

1. Bruises
2. Fractured and broken toes
3. Twists and sprains
4. Abrasions and cuts
5. Jumper's knee
6. Skin rashes
7. Minor concussions
8. Bloody noses
9. Muscle pulls and muscle strains
10. Muscle soreness or tightness

As I say to people, "It ain't Zumba!" You do get roughed up and banged up. You learn to almost...well...*enjoy* it after a while. You also learn that most of these minor injuries are really not all that bad.

One thing you can't believe is that you can just "take it easy" in class to avoid being injured. Not only will this rob you of the true training experience but odds are you'll actually line yourself up more towards getting hurt trying to avoid getting hurt.

Tip #5: Don't get frustrated

> *"To conquer frustration, one must remain intensely focused on the outcome, not the obstacles."*
> — T.F. Hodge

It's hard picking up new things that are very challenging. The amount you perceive you have yet to learn can be absolutely overwhelming and the truth is it's actually a lot more than that! I find that it takes very little time to get the major movements down but the subtle details take a great deal longer. To get it ingrained in your muscle memory and to develop useful reflexes and reactions, even longer. But know that it isn't a race; you are in class to train and make mistakes. In general, it takes everyone the same amount of time to pick up these techniques and instructors know that students don't learn things perfectly in one class.

It is essential that you take it a day at a time and do your best. Everything will fall into place over time and you need the patience to let it happen.

Tip #6: Don't compare your performance or endurance to others

Look in the mirror. That's your competition.

All too often you might find yourself looking around class, watching your fellow students and wondering why you aren't as good as that guy over there. Always remember, you should only be concerned about how you are improving based on *your own past performance* and that's it. You are your own yard stick because everyone is different. We all progress at our own rate and with our own strengths and weaknesses.

Maybe you'll find yourself wondering why someone got a belt when *you* feel they aren't qualified or deserving of the rank. This kind of thinking will lead to frustration every time and it's counter-productive. Nothing good comes out of it. If someone gets a belt, congratulate them. It was earned according to your instructors and your school's standards. If you are that bothered by it happening (or happening too often) then you might reconsider if your school is right for you.

Tip #7: Continue exercise outside of class

If you're like many, you'll limit your exercise to class time and that's it. To be successful, especially higher up the ranks, it is essential to keep up with an exercise regimen outside of class. After all, we are really only spending 2 - 4 hours a week in class. There's no way to fit a meaningful curriculum and a *complete* physical program in that short a time. The more you can squeeze into your busy schedule between classes (i.e., jogging, weightlifting, sit-ups, push-ups, stretching, walking), the better off you'll ultimately be.

Find a partner if you need to. That way you can keep each other honest as you push yourself to greater heights. Every student I admire in my school is an avid fitness junky. They lift weights or run on their "off" days or they go for swims or weightlift. These are the elite students of the school.

As for me, I take kickboxing, run, and train in Muay Thai when not training Krav Maga. These keep me not only more fit but also add even more variety to my exercise and training routine, keeping things interesting and stressing my body in different and otherwise challenging ways.

Tip #8: It will be tougher than any other physical regimen you've experienced

> *"Mental toughness is many things and rather difficult to explain. Its qualities are sacrifice and self-denial. Also, most importantly, it is combined with a perfectly disciplined will that refuses to give in. It's a state of mind-you could call it character in action."*
> *- Vince Lombardi*

If you are reading this and haven't yet started your first class, you are in for a challenge. Regardless of what kind of sport you've played or what kinds of fitness classes you've taken before, odds are Krav Maga is far and away the most intense physical and mental undertaking you've ever experienced. And it never gets easier. It will push your limits every class and drive you to give 100% at all times.

To succeed, it will require incredible amounts of dedication and persistence and every drop of fuel in your tank.

Tip #9: This is Reality Based Self-Defense, not an aerobics class

My instructor is fond of saying, "If you want a good workout you should consider cardio kickboxing. Here, you'll get fit but it's all about self-defense." Fitness comes, for sure, but the focus of the class is self-defense, all out aggression and getting down and dirty. I've heard it described before as fighting like a wet cat. That's the kind of attitude to have in training!

Tip #10: Sparring is essential so embrace it

"I had to get up and run in the morning for 2 hours, go to the gym and also get good opponents as sparring partners because I'm a big believer in that how you train is how you will fight at least when it came to me that's how it worked."
- Alexis Arguello

Most people shy away from sparring, giving reasons that they don't like roasting in the gear, they don't like the concept, etc. It's likely because they don't like getting hit. No one does, especially at first. Sparring is essential for learning distances, practicing combos, building fight endurance, and yes – taking a hit and staying calm.

Sparring isn't some macho display, nor is it meant to introduce a sport aspect to Krav Maga. It's meant to provide an opportunity to apply techniques to a dynamic, adrenaline-drenched situation. It's also meant to build up stamina in your muscles and increase your mental toughness and "fight IQ" (your smarts in selecting – in a split-second – the proper techniques, given your situation and opponent distance).

If you are scared to spar, that's good, you're normal. You need to push yourself past your limits because that's where the growth is and the results happen. To put yourself out there and spar whenever it's offered is to be part of the minority who do what it takes to get ahead and be their best, regardless of the pain, embarrassment, and fear.

You won't be sparring on your first day, and maybe not even your first several weeks, but as you do, there are some important principles to keep in mind.

I don't pretend to be an expert in sparring, just an enthusiast who has had great teachers, tries to learn from his many mistakes, and pays attention. The vast majority of these pointers come from the very talented instructors I've had the privilege of training under. The other few are my personal observations, usually as a result of doing the opposite and paying the price.

My experience so far has been Krav Maga sparring and Sityodtong Muay Thai. Even though some techniques differ, I haven't distinguished in my tips between one and the other.

Here are some principles to keep in mind:

- Hands up, keep your head moving, and keep your chin down. This one is hard to control. I know it trips me up a lot. But I've been told time and again that this is key to avoiding head shots or, in cases where you take a head shot, absorbing much of the impact. It's not usually the actual blow that staggers you so much as the whiplash of your head being knocked back and forth, side to side. Incidentally, this is usually how concussions happen and, surprisingly, it doesn't take as much impact as you think.

- Master your emotions. This applies to sparring as well as core self-defense. It is easy to let your emotions take you over and hinder your judgment, reflexes, and control ("Hit me, huh?! I'll show *you*!"). When sparring, particularly when getting whacked in the head, thumped in the side, or smashed in the nose, it is easy for emotions to flare up — anger, frustration, disappointment, etc. These will lead to dumb moves and emotional fighting. Not only that, this kind of emotional flare up can cause a friendly sparring match to escalate to a real fight with your opponent if you're not careful. Stay in tune with these emotions, feel them, acknowledge them, and let them go. Don't let them drive your reaction into something you're going to regret. Everyone gets hit, everyone has a good plan go to crap, and everyone has to adapt. Control your emotions so they don't control you!

- Speed trumps power in most cases. Don't go in with powerful attacks all the time. It's normal to think that every shot has to be the showstopper but this tires you quickly and irritates your partner. No one wins.

- Each match, expect to get your "bell rung" at least a few times by some good shots from your opponent. When it does, resist the urge to get angry or frustrated. This, out of all tips, is one of the hardest for more junior sparrers to control. We're hard-wired to lash out when we get hit. Our tempers flare and we get a squirt of adrenaline to feed the fire. We all have to learn to control the urge and learn that it's part of the drill.

- Don't trade blows. Use your brains and look for opportunities. Trading blows is just a mindless Fight Club.

- If you are nailed with a kick, don't automatically kick back (same goes for punches). This is a very common reaction people have when first starting out. On the other hand, if your opponent is falling victim to this urge, by all means, use it against them.

- Try to be unpredictable. It's easy to fall into obvious patterns when you are not thinking. Keep thinking to avoid going into predicable auto-pilot mode.

- Stay light-footed, not rooted in one place, and quick — move around and stay away from those blows. It's very tempting to just plant yourself and wait for your opponent to come to you. You get so focused on offensive and defensive moves that you forget your feet. More experienced opponents will take advantage of this and dance all around you, tenderizing you with blows from all sides. Remember to stay on your toes and don't lumber around flat-footed. Not doing so makes it tough to be quick and to avoid blows. For bigger folk like me, this is a tall order. Staying on ones toes for any length of time, bopping around in a sparring match, can be hard to focus on and tiring. If you don't though, you won't have the springiness to move around with the quickness you need.

- Control the distance and you control the fight. It is very hard for anyone but the experienced to know your short, mid, and long range zones and which weapons of your arsenal are appropriate in a sparring match. Sure, you can intellectualize it and apply it in drills but when it comes down to a dynamic sparring match, especially when you're getting pummeled, it is easier said than done. Nevertheless, if you can do this, the match is far more likely to be in your favor.

- Know your distances and zones. Following on the heels of the last tip, don't kick in a punch zone and vice versa.

- Stay loose, don't clench up and get tense. If there is one thing everyone does when they first start sparring it's to get very tense. This will tire you out early and actually make the hits you take more painful. Learn to loosen up and it will help tremendously. An easy way to apply this is to pay attention to your shoulders at the beginning of the round. More than likely they are hunched up. Drop them and stay relaxed.

- Don't decide ahead of time what your attack will be. Let your opponents show you what to go after by observing what he/she is not defending. One cannot defend all targets at once.

- Accept the fact that *everyone gets hit*. There's no shame. You are not being judged harshly by people watching as you might think. Surprisingly, more often than not, getting hit doesn't hurt as much as you imagine, especially with sparring gear strapped on.

- When you miss a shot, you get surprised by a hit, or something doesn't go as you planned DO NOT get frustrated and start obsessing about it. Let it go. There's time to analyze things after the match. If you get hung up on these things you are distracted and your performance will degrade rapidly.

- After landing blows on your opponent, get out of there. Don't wait for retaliation and don't expect your hit to shut them down. If you land punches and/or kicks you have to remember that you are now in their striking range too! Throw your attack or attacks and move out of there.

- I was told by a well-known Muay Thai coach once that amateurs move forward and backward, pros move side to side. Very good advice and one of my favorite tips.

- As you continue to spar into the future try not to stay with the same partner. Many people find buddies in class and stick with them for all bouts and training. Big mistake. After a while you learn to adapt to each other's style and you get lazy. New opponents teach you new things and keep you on your toes. Once in a while, try to spar with someone better than you. Provided that they have the right attitude, this can help your technique quite a bit. Not to mention keeping your ego in check!

- No one likes a cheap shot or a cry baby. Remain professional even if your opponent is not behaving that way. If you don't you'll have a harder and harder time finding sparring partners.

- Let your power be proportional to your opponent. If you are a large person, for example, and get rotated into a match with a much smaller person, don't be a jerk and knock their head off with a kick.

- Alternate your high and low attacks to confuse your opponent. For example, kicking then following up with a high shot like a jab/cross. When people get kicked low their brain focuses on the body below the belt and vice versa for the head. You can capitalize on this tendency by alternating your attacks. Not predictably of course because, done too many times, even the most dense opponent will catch on to your ploy.

- Manage your fight speed to control your opponent's speed. I was shown recently that you can lull your opponent into a slower pace by dropping your pace, appearing tired or sleepy. Their brain automatically drops down a gear too. Same goes for speeding up. So if you come in with a flurry and drop down a few gears your opponent likely will too, allowing you to spring back in high speed and surprise them. Try it.

- As you become more experienced, you can try to rotate through your sparring styles to keep your opponent guessing. Bangkok, Tiger, and Boxer styles were demonstrated a few weeks ago in class as classic styles of Muay Thai sparring. Each is very different in approach. We were told that rotating between these various styles will certainly keep your sparring partner on their toes and keep them guessing. Lots of training goes into being able to be proficient in any of these styles, let alone all three, but the point is valid even for people new to sparring — keep your style fluid and open to the many possibilities out there.

- There is no winner in sparring. This is training and you shouldn't be "duking it out", hoping to "win". This is to get better and work on your technique and fight endurance. Treat it that way.

- Learn the techniques for sparring opponents taller, shorter, and of the same height as you. Odds are that you will be sparring mostly people who are shorter or taller than you are. Regardless of the height difference there are techniques and modes that come into play for opponents depending on how they stack up against your height. If you are on the taller side of things, for example, you will often need to let your opponent come to you. If you are shorter than your opponent, you will often need to get inside their defenses for more in-fighting. Knowing how to adapt will bring you more success as one set of techniques will not fit all matches.

- Lastly, try to get better every time. You're there to learn and to get better, not to get beat up or pummel others to a pulp.

Tip #11: It never *ever* gets easier

There's a myth among some that the higher you go, the easier it gets. This applies to cardio as well as drills and learning techniques. It's simply not true. No matter what level you are, you should be pushing yourself past your limits. So whether you are out of shape and just starting or celebrating your 10th successive year in training, you should be at the same level of exhaustion at the end of class. Getting in better shape merely means that you have to push yourself harder, not take it easier.

I admire the people in class who, even though they have been at this for a long time, are panting on the edge of passing out and dripping sweat mid-way through class. They push themselves to their absolute breaking point. They don't care who's watching, who's judging, or even if they pass out or puke. They are committed and they are going to give themselves a challenge no matter what. I love being in class with this kind of student. They inspire me and make me want to be my best too.

Tip #12: True motivation comes from within

"They can conquer who believe they can."
- Ralph Waldo Emerson

Self-help books are useful, motivational posters are entertaining and give food for thought, and discussions with fellow students can build confidence and help cement your determination but in the end the true motivation comes from *within*. Yeah, it sounds corny but it truly has to be your drive and your goals have to be *your goals*. You have to want to succeed for you and only for you. This is your journey and you are the participant and the benefactor of every minute of training.

Virtually every student who has dropped out of training has done so because they lacked the internal motivation to continue. Every Black Belt you see had the passion, the drive, the goals, and the motivation to stick with it, day in and day out, class after class, injury after injury, to make it to where they needed to be.

If you want to succeed you have to have the will and determination to succeed. No instructor, spouse, or fellow classmate can keep you in it for the long haul.

Tip #13: Favor speed and aggression over power and technique

There's an old saying often attributed to Mark Twain: "It's not the size of the dog in the fight, it's the size of the fight in the dog." I couldn't agree more. It's usually the most vicious, rabid lunatic who walks away from an altercation. Technique and power always need to be there but without aggression and speed it's all for nothing. This is counter to many new students' beliefs. In fact, watch an inexperienced person sparring. Every kick and punch is their knockout punch. They lack finesse and don't yet understand the range of weapons and the variety of attacks they can bring. More experienced students have power for sure, but also know the importance of getting inside quick, attacking like a viper when the opportunity presents itself.

In self-defense situations, speed and aggression are paramount. If you have a powerhouse knockout punch but your attacker is on you an instant before you can land it – what good is it? If your attacker is more aggressive and is fighting like a wet cat while you are trying to form a perfect stance – who wins?

So keep this one in mind and it will serve you well in your training. Try to develop speed and know where that 'On/Off' switch is for your aggression. You'll need it every class.

Tip #14: There will be casualties

Maybe you've heard it before. There is a ridiculously high drop-out rate in martial arts. Krav Maga is grueling and intense, far more intense than many people realize. I heard recently that, statistically, third degree Black Belts are 3 in 10,000. If you are one of the few that sticks it out and goes the distance, you can be sure that a great many of the friends you make in the beginning months will drop off in the first year.

Tip #15: You MUST drink plenty of fluids

This is especially true if you are overweight as I was starting out. You are going to sweat a *lot*, regardless of the time of year, and much of the moisture you lose will be from your breath. As you pant and try to catch your breath throughout the class you'll be losing massive amounts of water and bringing your body to the danger zone. Stay on top of it and keep hydrated. If not, you'll end up with a migraine and nausea, possibly throwing up – or worse, ending up with heat stroke or heat exhaustion.

In terms of the kinds of fluid you should drink, water is great and should be consumed in abundance. You can consider sports drinks as well, though I've personally grown less enamored with these over the years.

The thing with fluids that I've found is that you are going to be far better off hydrating *before* your class than only drinking a lot *during* and *after* class. This is because your body takes some time to process the fluid and many of us don't drink enough during the day to begin with. So what you want to do if you aren't the kind of person who drinks as much as they should (e.g., pretty much everyone on the planet) is to start drinking sips of water a few hours before class. Don't chug but rather take a swallow or two every few minutes in the hours leading up to class. If you drink too fast you'll get a stomachache and your body won't even bother trying to process it all; it will just pass right through you. You want to take the water in slowly so it has time to stick around in your system. While we're on the subject, your pee should be light straw color before running out the door to hit class. Anything darker than that and you're flirting with disaster.

Tip #16: Later on, you'll see that even lower belts have something to teach

Know that, as you advance, you should never let your belt, rank, or position in the school go to your head. Everyone is a lifelong student and your higher rank means that you got around to starting your journey before the lower belts did.

That said, be extremely cautious in pointing things out to more advanced belts as you just start out. Some people take feedback better than others while some people are downright annoyed if they are corrected or otherwise critiqued by a White Belt. I found it best as an underbelt to focus my energy on observing and trying to keep my big mouth shut. In fact, I still do that. Do what feels right for you in the moment but be sensitive to how others might react.

Tip #17: Use your belt as a goal but don't obsess about it

If your school uses belts, you'll find that they are helpful milestones to strive for but nothing to lose sleep over. Some people dismiss the concept of belts altogether and say Krav Maga has patches or nothing at all. As I said earlier, a quick internet image search for Imi Lichtenfeld will readily show him wearing a belt. Same with Darren Levine, one of his few students still practicing in the States.

I like belts as goals. I think they are a physical representation of my hard work. I don't obsess about them but when I do achieve a belt I am proud. I worked hard for it. However you feel about belts, patches, or whatever else your school chooses, is up to you. But however you do it, consider setting some goals to keep yourself engaged and rewarded through the process. Otherwise it becomes not much different than going to the gym.

Tip #18: Buy equipment right the first time

Prior to starting martial arts I thought surely martial arts must be kind of cheap when it came to sports equipment. Little did I know the kinds of training weapons, clothing, pads, cups, guards, and other gear I'd need to pick up as a practitioner. It's certainly not like racing a Formula One car in your free time but it's pretty pricey nonetheless.

My advice in this category (and I know it's tough starting out) is to not skimp if there's any way to avoid it. By buying cheap you'll think you're saving money, only to have to buy the good alternative later on down the road because the cheap version failed so quickly. "Buy it nice so you don't buy it twice."

Generally speaking, and this does vary school to school so please check with them, you need some of the following equipment starting out:

- Good quality gear bag – the bigger, the better
- Decent mouthguard (buy two and fit them carefully). *Boil and bite* are fine but as you get more experienced and it appears you are in it for the long haul, you might consider a professionally-fitted one from your dentist.
- Shoes if your school allows them and you want to train in them
- Boxing gloves (usually 16 oz. but check with your school)
- MMA gloves. I like grappling gloves because they cover more of your thumb
- "Glove dogs" for your boxing gloves
- Shin guards
- Belly protector
- Training gun

- Training knife

Again, your mileage may vary so be sure to check with your school for their requirements.

Tip #19: Be gracious

Whenever you receive help, be thankful for it. Be thankful for your instructors as well. Although they are getting paid to do what they do, you must always be grateful for their expertise, patience, and passion for helping you get better. Be gracious also to your fellow students for whatever help they might offer.

Tip #20: Don't talk smack about people

As you progress, regardless of your attitude, you'll likely be tempted to trash talk about people. This partner was bossy. This one was sloppy. That one has weak punches. The urge can be strong to bad mouth people after class when you're all amped up on adrenaline, especially if they screwed you over somehow in class. My advice to you is to clamp down hard on that urge and try to take the high road. It is fun to trash talk and it relieves a lot of frustration and anger but schools are small environments and, like it or not, many of you are in it together for the long haul.

Tip #21: You will lose weight but only if you make it a lifestyle commitment

In my first year training in Krav Maga, I busted my butt. To my surprise, I only lost 10 pounds. Where were all these weight loss results I was promised when I started? I was burning over 1200 calories per hour with each class. What happened?

Well, what happened was I wasn't making it a lifestyle change. Sure, I was burning those calories but it was only two to three times a week. As soon as I left I'd continue eating like a pig and not tracking my calories (calories in vs. out). That was my problem.

About a year and a half into my training I decided that I couldn't outrun a bad diet and made the decision to make it an around-the-clock concern. I tracked my calories and fitness and took the lifestyle seriously. Sure enough, the weight began to melt away. I was losing 5 pounds or more a week. In six months, I lost 40 pounds more. In five more months, I lost a further 25 pounds. In total, I am down more than 100 pounds today.

The point here is not to brag but to set your expectations realistically so you can go into it with eyes wide open if you're looking to lose weight. Make fitness a priority in your life, exercise vigorously four or five times a week, and track your calories. That will be your key.

Tip #22: There will always be someone better than you

No matter how good you get, no matter how long you train, no matter how dedicated you are, no matter how often you go to class, there will always be someone better, faster, more experienced, stronger, and more skilled than you. Always.

You can choose to view that as depressing and demotivating or do what I do: consider that a great advantage. To know that there are people nearby who have more to offer in certain areas than you should be a comfort.

Tip #23: It takes a lot of commitment

When I first started training, due to my schedule and other activities, I knew I wasn't able to train more than twice a week. I was assured at the time that that was more than sufficient. Even though I was doubtful I went ahead and trained twice a week, and continued that way for the first nine months. I saw some results but, in retrospect, now that I am training about four or five times a week, I realize that I would have gotten a lot more out of my basic training had I had the ability to go more often.

Regardless of how fit you are, how quickly you pick things up, or how young you may be, to be successful and make substantial progress, you need to train no less than *two to three times a* week. Optimally, I shoot for four times if at all possible and, if it's possible for you, I would suggest you do the same as often as you can. The more you train, the more progress you'll see, the more dedication you'll demonstrate to your classmates and instructors, and obviously the more fit you'll become.

Tip #24: Never let your 'good' be your 'best'

Good is the enemy of Great. It's easy to become complacent. When you train long enough, it can be tempting to start letting your good enough become your best. You have to be aware of this and fight it. Every class should be your best class. You have to learn to never stop pushing yourself, to never feel comfortable.

Remember that feeling during the first few classes – the feeling of inadequacy, humility, terror, of not feeling up to the challenge. Try to bottle that up inside for later use and take a sip of it before every class. Bring yourself down to earth and remind yourself that you must never find a level and coast. You can't ever let yourself reach a level and believe yourself entitled to respect. You have to always remember these initial days and weeks of training and carry a bit of that forward into the future to keep you grounded.

Tip #25: Don't go looking for fights

This is one of the most important tips and could avoid you getting hurt, jailed, or even killed. It's common for students to let their training go to their heads early on. Within a few classes people often think they're indestructible, capable of handling gangs of thugs like in the movies. It's unfortunate that this happens and I often wonder how many people get their butts kicked as a result of this false belief. The fact is, we are not proficient in Krav Maga or any other martial art with only a few classes. It's my belief that it takes many months before someone can be capable to defend themselves effectively in the real world against real thugs.

Therefore, don't leave your first class and start looking for dark alleys to test your newfound skills. Don't start going to seedy bars and asking the biggest biker, "You lookin' at me?!" Don't go to the dark side of town and bump into thugs and try to start a fight. You may think you're invincible with some training under your belt but it's not foolproof and it doesn't make you invincible.

Even after years of training, your body a human weapon, your muscles taught cords of steel, your first option should be to avoid conflict and your second should be to run. You should never use your skills unless absolutely necessary and you should never be one to provoke attacks.

Tip #26: This isn't an action movie with you in the starring role

It's easy to get punch drunk with the power you feel in class. You must remember that you are not, however, performing in some secret action movie where you are the star. That's how I see some fellow students; there's no other explanation for their behavior in class. They think themselves as movie stars and the Krav Maga class is their movie. All sparring and self-defense moves have thunderous sound effects going off in their heads. They imagine themselves Special Forces or Jason Bourne, whacking and chopping enemy combatants with ruthless efficiency, strutting the floor while their boyfriend or girlfriend is watching from the sidelines, gob-smacked with adoration.

If you are thinking like this, the best thing to do is to stop. You are learning self-defense. You are getting in better shape, physically and emotionally. You are meeting new friends and learning about how to survive a violent street encounter. Any resemblance to an action hero, living or dead, is purely coincidental and should therefore be dismissed immediately before you get caught up in acting like a fool.

Tip #27: You are stronger than you think

If you are just starting out, you are embarking on a very arduous journey. There's no way for me to impress upon you how physically demanding it is to train in Krav Maga. Like trying to describe what a lemon tastes like to a three year-old, it's just something you have to experience for yourself.

But know this: you are far stronger than you believe yourself to be. Even if you think you are capable of any feat right now, you will be in a situation early on in your training where you are questioning your sanity, your strength, and your ability to make it to the end of the class. We've all been there and we all continue to find ourselves there, week after week. Know that you are stronger and have a deep power reserve that is yours for the taking if you learn how to dig deep and never give up.

Tip #28: You will only get out of it what you put into it

This, of all the tips contained in this Guide, might be my most closely held Krav Maga belief. There are legions of students around the world who train in Krav Maga and happen to suffer the delusion that they are actually giving their all in class. As you look around you may notice them. They go through the motions in class and are utterly convinced that they are fully committed but the reality is they are not connecting with the training and executing the moves in a savage, fighting cat, "kill or be killed" sort of manner. This leads to half-assed techniques, an incomplete understanding, and in the end, ineffective self-defense. That's dangerous.

When you immerse yourself in the training, adopt the right mindset, understand the practicality of the techniques (i.e., how they would be used), know your distances, go all out, leave training exhausted and better than you left training last time then you will be getting the most out of your training.

Tip #29: It's never too soon to wear your cup

It never ceases to amaze me how many students refuse to wear a cup in class. There are endless excuses:

- "I haven't gotten around to it"
- "I forgot mine"
- "I'm going Commando today"

…but they all vanish into thin air as soon as someone gets slammed in the groin – this is Krav Maga training, after all. Lisa Simpson famously said in an episode of The Simpsons TV show, "No groin, no Krav Maga!"

Probably the top excuse I've heard is that groin cups are uncomfortable. Listen, no matter how uncomfortable a cup is to wear, it pales in comparison to how it feels to take a palm strike, kick, or heel strike to the groin, believe me. This is the 21st century where, believe it or not, you can get your hands on cups that actually aren't that bad. *Diamond MMA* and *Nutty Buddy* athletic cups are two brands that are quite comfortable and designed for high-impact sports and activities. Look around and make the investment in a quality cup.

It would be one thing if it was behavior that just affected the people who refused to wear cups but the truth of the matter is that it affects others in class too. In other words, if you know you partner isn't wearing a cup, you will alter your *combatives* when going after them. I hear frequently from instructors ready to demo a technique on a student to show the class, "Are you wearing a cup?" This annoys me almost as much as that student answering, "No." Sometimes a little voice inside my head can be heard to whisper, "Hit him in the groin and teach him to wear his cup!"

Recently I heard a fellow student said that he wears his groin cup to school bake sales. Wiser words were never said that day.

Wear your dang cup!

Tip #30: Eat before class to fuel your workout

I don't mean hitting Taco Bell on the way to class. I mean good, healthy food that will nourish your body and won't make you gassy or weigh you down. A small to medium-sized bowl of oatmeal with some fruit or honey is a winning choice for me. Maybe some rice and veggies, a protein or granola bar, some whole grain cereal or toast, or a banana. Shake it up but keep it easy, fast, and healthy.

Whatever you settle on, make sure you're not eating it immediately before class. Ninety minutes to an hour is typically cited as the best amount of time to give your body to work it into the system. I would even suggest closer to two hours prior if you can. Any closer to class than that and you'll be having all sorts of trouble like cramps, nausea, gas, and some pretty horrified fellow students standing around you and looking nervously in your direction.

Tip #31: Cut your nails

After you get gouged by someone's claws in class you'll quickly realize how important this one truly is. Not only is this painful but it can easily result in infections.

Take a good look at your nails in class, making a mental note to trim them after your shower should they need it. Also, get in the habit of taking a look at the beginning of the day after your morning shower too. If you try to do this once in a while the odds are that you'll usually avoid being Wolverine in class, raking your partners and flaying their skin from their bones with every combative you perform on them.

Tip #32: Adopt a habit of being meticulously clean

You need to make a conscious decision to be scrupulously clean when it comes to Krav Maga. This applies to your body as well as your gear. Clean Krav Maga practitioners are happy practitioners that people don't mind partnering with. *Don't be a walking biohazard!* My rule of thumb is to be squeaky clean walking in and keep your gear so clean that you could eat a sandwich off it.

Dirty equipment, besides being rank and smelly, doesn't last nearly as long and harbors mold, mildew, bacteria, and all sorts of nasty germs and viruses such as *E. coli*, *staph*, and *Molluscum contagiosum* that can lead you and innocent bystanders to athlete's foot, ringworm, rashes, MRSA, and warts.

Be aware also of touching your facial areas with your hands during class. Once class starts you should consider your body a weapon in more ways than one. Your body, especially your hands, are bacteria and germ-carrying and completely filthy. The surest, quickest way to get yourself infected or sick in the dojo is to start touching open orifices such as your mouth, nose, and eyes with your hands.

Although completely unavoidable in activities such as Krav Maga, you should be aware of the realities of skin-to-skin contact like catching Staphylococcus aureus (MRSA) or other nasty germs. This should not discourage you from engaging in techniques that involve skin-to-skin contact – let's face it, it happens almost constantly – but it should make you more aware so that you take proper precautions wherever you can: stay clean, avoid people who have rashes or are routinely unclean, and get "back to clean" as soon as you possibly can after class is over. When you are doing techniques that require someone to grab your face or eyes (or you likewise do the same to them), be aware of what's going on and try to minimize the chance of picking something up or passing something along. It's very tough, bordering on impossible, but a little awareness can go a long way.

I usually have a bottle of alcohol sanitizer hanging from my bag with some disinfectant wipes inside the bag to freshen up in between sweaty drills and especially after class. It's a good practice too – particularly if your dojo is a barefoot one – to wipe down your feet with a baby wipe after class. It's incredible when you stop to think about it the sheer number of stinky, nasty feet that slid across that very mat that you were just working out on.

Obviously wipes and sanitizers are no substitute for a shower or a date with the sink and a squirt of soap but they do in a pinch and should neutralize the majority of nastiness on your hands until you can get more serious about it. As soon as you get home, get out of those clothes and jump in the shower as soon as you can. If your school has showers you can choose to get clean even sooner but remember that you are potentially dealing with a lot more germs than at home.

Be sure to include your mouthguard and water bottle in your cleaning routine. I've known many people who just pop their mouthguard back in its case and toss it into their bag. This makes me shudder just thinking about it. Some folks just refill their water bottle over and over, week after week without giving it a thought that it might be getting nasty and germy. Mouthguards and water bottles are swarming with nasty germs and bacteria that only build up over time. Give them both a thorough washing, soaking your mouthguard in mouthwash, after every class.

Tip #33: If you get cut, bandage it up

If you get scratched or get a bloody nose during class, don't get all "macho" and ignore it, dribbling and spattering blood all over the place. An exposed wound is as dangerous to others as it is for you! An open wound is a two-way portal for germs and disease. If you are carrying something, you are exposing others to it. If one of the many students is carrying germs and left them behind on some equipment or the floor, you are wide open to let it in. Take care of any wound immediately. Right now, no excuses.

Although I get some weird reactions from people, I carry a small first aid kit with me in my bag. It contains alcohol wipes, bandages, swabs, ammonia salts, Liquid Bandage, tape (for buddy taping injured toes), and a few other items.

Any time I get a cut or scratch I immediately call "Time!" and head over to my bag to take care of it. Liquid Bandage does well as it seals the wound up pretty well and won't fall off like a bandage will. If you can take the industrial solvent smell of it, there really isn't anything better to get "sealed up" and back into action.

Tip #34: If you use community equipment, wipe it down when you're done

If you can, try to use as much of your own equipment as you are able. Understandably, it's very hard to do this when you're just starting out as you aren't yet "fully equipped". So, in the inevitable event that you do share, you'll discover that there are few worse things than grabbing a piece of equipment (i.e., a kick shield or Muay Thai pads) only to find it literally dripping with someone else's sweat. Completely nasty and very unsanitary.

When you're done with a drill – and you've done it correctly – your piece of equipment will be covered in your sweat. Do your duty and clean it up before stowing it away. Even if you are the only person doing this, do it. Others will notice and, at the very least, will admire your thoughtfulness. At best, people will follow suit and your dojo will become a cleaner, less germy place because of you.

Everyone thinks that germs come from someone else. That's true. But the deeper truth is that they come in one form or another from pretty much everyone – including you. As much as you'd like to think, you are not exempt. You are not bacteria, virus, or germ-free. Hold up your end of the bargain and keep these things to yourself.

If your dojo doesn't provide disinfectant sprays or wipes politely ask or, better yet, bring some of your own in your bag at all times.

Tip #35: Hang out a little after class

As I look back on it, some of the most valuable lessons I've received over the years came to me after class. That time when you're wiping down and gathering up your stuff, chatting it up with some fellow students, or maybe walking off the mat with an instructor or senior student.

It is after class, as you stuff equipment back into your gear bag, change out of your sweat-drenched shirt, and grab a protein bar that you can shoot the breeze and do a kind of *debrief* or *lessons learned* with fellow students. Maybe you talk with your partner frankly about your performance and ask about what they think you could improve. Perhaps you ask your instructor how you can improve.

Wherever the conversation heads or whoever you chat with, you'll find more often than not that it is very useful, enlightening, and a great way to form closer bonds with your fellow students, many of whom you may be training with a few times a week for years to come.

Tip #36: Temper your Reality-Based Self-Defense with some reality

Never think of Krav Maga as a be-all-end-all solution to keeping you safe. There are many legal and psychological ramifications to using Krav Maga in the real world and nearly all of them are extremely unpleasant.

Knowing what you can and cannot get away with in a self-defense situation, based on your local laws, is very important. Yes, it is "better to be judged by 12 than carried by 6". Always do what you have to do to get home safe. But, it is always best to be as informed as possible about the realities – and after-effects – of real-world self-defense to be as informed as possible. It's not all about bashing a nameless attacker into submission and walking away a hero. It's about avoiding conflict and dangerous situations or applying just enough force to get away in those times when a fight is unavoidable.

I suggest frequently reading up on the topic to stay current and to keep it in the forefront of your mind. Rory Miller is a great resource, for example, and has many great books and blog articles on the subject of the harsh realities of self-defense. I cannot recommend highly enough his book *Facing Violence: Preparing for the Unexpected*. Grab a copy, read it...then read it again.

Tip #37: Focus on what you're doing well instead of what you're doing poorly

As a new student, it can be very daunting just starting out, not only in your first class, but for weeks or even *months* after you start. It can be disheartening when you are counted amongst the most junior, inexperienced students in the class. Everything is so new and there's so much to learn, so many nuances to everything.

It's important when you feel like this to remember that it is essential to focus on what you're doing well, rather than what you aren't doing well. Let's face it, there's going to be a lot of room for improvement. Even things as basic as a punch are actually pretty involved when you get down to the finer details. Even after years of training it's not unusual to be working on refining your technique even further. So just imagine how overwhelming it can be when everything requires that kind of focus and body control.

The best thing to do is to focus on improving things here and there and celebrate the successes. If you do five pushups your first class and can't possibly do one more... then take class the next week and slam out six or seven? That's progress.

Focus on these small victories and learn to take solace in the fact that with hard work, focus, and dedication you will get better and more experienced. It happens one class at a time.

Tip #38: You've got to upgrade and downsize your body

Your body is your machine.

If you're like almost everyone else, you are coming to Krav Maga carrying a few extra pounds and maybe not the best shape of your life. You can relax; you're not alone. In fact, in my experience, many people join Krav Maga with the explicit goal of losing weight. I know I did.

People often get lulled into thinking that, because they are busting their butts in class, the weight will take care of itself or that they are "fat fit". I fell squarely into this category as do most overweight people who've been at it for years. They become content with their bodies and feel that things are just "good enough".

The problem with this is that your Krav Maga effectiveness is directly tied to your body condition. Sounds obvious, I know, but this eludes a lot of students. Many people continue along with their "good enough" body. They tire easier, their flexibility suffers and, in hauling so much unnecessary weight around with them, they put more strain on their lungs, heart, and joints than they need to. Their bodies are machines and the more tuned up the machine, the better it runs.

So, if you are in the situation where you are starting Krav Maga to lose some weight, do yourself a favor and make martial arts a lifestyle choice for you. Don't obsess about it night and day and only live off chicken and rice. But string your classes together with a healthy lifestyle, making conscious, healthy decisions with your life outside of class. Your body will reward you with a more efficient machine for Krav Maga.

Tip #39: Be willing to accept critiques and feedback

"All effective and engaging learning experiences provide frequent and meaningful feedback. Without feedback on whether or not one is getting closer to a goal, progress is unlikely."
- Anonymous

It's hard for some people to accept feedback, even from an instructor. It's important to remember how important feedback is in getting better. Even when we think we are doing something perfectly, we can only get one perspective on it if we shut ourselves off to feedback – that is, our own. The problem with this is that often our own judgment, ego, and view on a particular technique we are executing is biased or, at best, pretty limited. That's why having an "extra pair of eyes" or an objective view on our performance can be so crucial, especially from someone more experienced than ourselves.

When you are starting out and for the remainder of your time training you will do yourself a huge favor if you'll keep an open mind and listen to whatever feedback comes your way. You can internalize it, process it, evaluate it, and determine what you think about it, rejecting it or accepting it as you feel fit. But you should always go through this process when you are lucky enough to get feedback from anyone. It's what will allow you to improve your performance by leaps and bounds, far faster than just following your internal voice; you know, the one that only has nice things to say about you!

The other aspect about feedback to understand is captured so well in that old adage: "Everyone's a Teacher, Everyone's a Student". This doesn't mean that all students should have their spotlight in front of the class. Rather, it means that no matter who you are interacting with, there is always a lesson taking place, even if someone is also a junior student or even if someone isn't formally "teaching" you. If you are perceptive, you will notice lessons all around you, even if they are lessons in what not to do and how not to act.

The flip side of this is that you, even as a beginner student, are a teacher. You are a human who perceives things around you and processes it through your own lenses. You have valuable interpretations of events and can mirror things back to people, providing feedback and insight that others might have missed. I'm not referring to critiquing but honest feedback. Critiquing has a tone of judgment; feedback is more insightful and is designed to help the person you are providing it to. Provide feedback sparingly in your beginner years and with careful judgment as not to offend anyone. Some people don't take kindly to junior students providing feedback so use your discretion.

Tip #40: Leave your ego at the door

Maybe you're a successful millionaire who vacations at their villa in the Hamptons. Maybe you own your own successful construction company. Perhaps you're an A-List actor in Hollywood who just wrapped his latest movie. Whatever your situation outside of the school, leave it at the door. In class, you are a student. Just like everyone else.

You may be king of your castle and master of your domain from nine to five but you can't allow that to follow you into class. You need a certain amount of humility to be successful and if you think your title or outside successes grant you special privileges or set you somehow higher up the food chain than your fellow students, you've got a rude awakening waiting for you.

Tip #41: Choose partners wisely and mix it up

Krav Maga is not a solo sport. Despite being designed for personal self-defense it is often practiced with a partner and you'll find that few things can mess up your training more than ending up with the wrong partner. A partner is not someone who just holds pads, succumbs to (or administers) the technique of the moment, or someone opposite you who's waiting their turn. They are an integral part of your training and their importance cannot be overstated.

I've had bad partners, good partners, and phenomenal partners. If a partner's no good you run the risk of being barraged with meaningless/inaccurate critiques, getting injured, not learning the techniques being focused on that day, getting frustrated, and constantly having to readjust yourself to accommodate your partner's shortcomings. All of these make for a horrible training session. True, there's something you can salvage from even these sessions but, having been through a fair share of bad ones myself, I'd just as soon not have to be in that position if it can be avoided. Hey, I'm here to learn and have only so many sessions per week to get it right so why not make each minute really count?

A good partner, on the other hand, ups your game. I've been pushed beyond what I thought I was capable of, learned lessons better than I originally heard them described, and been elevated to higher levels of excellence with the right partner. They make training more fun, a great learning experience, and mentally and physically exhausting. We come to the end of class and I want to keep going!

When it's time to get a partner in our school we hear those same words: "PARTNER UP!" It's then that people scramble to pair with a fellow student for the next segment of class. Some people, myself included, will sometimes ask a student before class if they'd care to partner up that class, while others might wing it. Some people go with the same partners they always use, a dangerous thing; I'll get to that in a second. Occasionally, someone will be the last guy picked, without a partner, standing up and looking around for a warm body to pair up with. I hate being in that position. Once the dust settles, like it or not, you're stuck with your partner and you have to make the best of it.

Being a good partner involves the following:

- Always trying your hardest at all times. This is tough for some people. When some partners are not 'up' (i.e. not working the technique on the partner) they think it's "not their turn" and get distracted. Maybe they don't put their fullest into it. This is obnoxious no matter how you slice it.

- When it's time for pad-holding you are training just as the striker is so don't check out on your partner. Proper pad holding helps work your defense and, if done right, is extremely tiring on the arms and core. You're cheating your partner and yourself if you wuss out on pad holding. Here's how I feel proper pad holding feels: hold up the pads at the proper height, fairly close together — not touching but not too far apart either. Now, imagine someone applying pressure on one pad, pressing in hard trying to push it back. You resist to keep the pad from moving much by pushing back. Next, imagine that the pressure is not constant but rather a second or so of pressure then release — like, say, a punch or an elbow, right? That's what your pad-holding should be like. When the blow comes in you should meet it, feeding the pads to your partner. Don't jam them but provide a healthy counter-pressure to simulate hitting an opponent. Without this counter-pressure you will have your pads flying back out of control and almost guarantee your partner and yourself getting injured.

- If you feel compelled to correct your partner or point out something in need of their attention, do so in a respectful way, never in an arrogant or condescending fashion. Feedback is essential to getting better but just being an ass about it is only going to alienate your partner.

- This is Krav Maga. Keep things very aggressive and violent but don't let this override the need to train safely. Rough up your partner but don't injure them. Injuries keep people from training and word spreads about how bad people train. In fact, you can often tell the psychotics and sociopaths in class because they are often the ones referred to above that are usually picked last, left to stand alone bellowing, "ANYONE NEED A PARTNER!?"

- Mix it up. People who use the same partner time and time again are seen as very "cliquey" and act above everyone else. Not only that but I think this is more dangerous than ending up with a lame duck partner. You end up getting to know your partner too well and it can dampen your game considerably over time. You become too comfortable and complacent. This is bad because, to succeed, you need to reduce predictability in your training. Lastly, rotating partners gives you a chance to know your team better, broadening your friendships. Remember, for the ones like you who are in this for the long haul, you'll be seeing an awful lot of them for a long time. Might as well know who they are, right?

- If you are female, strongly consider partnering with males regularly. As intimidating as that can be, odds are that – if you are going to ever be attacked on the street – it will most likely be a man who's the attacker. If you've never gone toe to toe with a man in training, how on earth can you expect to defend against a man? That's like learning to deep-sea dive on dry land.

Tip #42: Have fun!

Lastly, if you look at Krav Maga merely as a workout, something to be dreaded or even nervous about, you will probably not last too long. It's really hard but you should have fun. Embrace the concepts and enjoy it.

It's the most fun getting smacked around you'll ever have.

Your Turn

So that's it. But I want to be 100% sure that I've given you information that can help you. I put forth my take on the kinds of things people might have if they are just starting out or if they are seriously considering taking up Krav Maga but there's no way I can accurately predict everything that is on everyone's mind.

So this is your opportunity to ask me what's on your mind. If I didn't cover an aspect that you were expecting or you had questions about anything contained in this Guide, this is your open invitation to reach out and ask me.

You can contact me at kravmagajourney@gmail.com. Drop me a line and ask away. I promise to do my best to answer as soon as possible and answer what's on your mind.

Cheat Sheet

Tip #1: Stay open-minded

Tip #2: Don't bring in baggage

Tip #3: Be receptive to other people

Tip #4: You will get hurt

Tip #5: Don't get frustrated

Tip #6: Don't compare your performance or endurance to others, only yourself

Tip #7: Continue exercise outside of class

Tip #8: It will be tougher than any other physical regimen you've experienced

Tip #9: This is Reality Based Self-Defense, not an aerobics class

Tip #10: Sparring is essential so embrace it

Tip #11: It never ever gets easier

Tip #12: True motivation has to come from within

Tip #13: Favor speed and aggression over power and technique

Tip #14: There will be casualties

Tip #15: You MUST drink plenty of fluids

Tip #16: As you move forward you'll see that even lower belts have something to teach

Tip #17: If your school uses belts, use your belt as a goal but don't obsess about it

Tip #18: Buy equipment right the first time

Tip #19: Be gracious

Tip #20: Don't talk smack about people

Tip #21: You will lose weight but only if you make it a lifestyle commitment

Tip #22: There will always be someone better than you

Tip #23: It takes a lot of commitment

Tip #24: Never let your 'good' be your 'best'

Tip #25: Don't go looking for fights

Tip #26: This isn't an action movie with you in the starring role

Tip #27: You are far stronger than you think

Tip #28: You will only get out of it what you put into it

Tip #29: It's never too soon to wear your cup!

Tip #30: Eat enough "good" food before class to fuel your workout

Tip #31: Cut your nails

Tip #32: Adopt a habit of being meticulously clean

Tip #33: If you get cut, bandage it up!

Tip #34: If you use community equipment, wipe it down when you're done

Tip #35: Hang out a little after class

Tip #36: Temper your Reality-Based Self-Defense with some reality

Tip #37: Focus on what you're doing well instead of what you're doing poorly

Tip #38: You've got to upgrade and downsize your body

Tip #39: Be willing to accept critiques and feedback

Tip #40: Leave your ego at the door

Tip #41: Choose partners wisely and mix it up

Tip #42: Have fun!

About the Author

Craig De Ruisseau is an enterprise systems architect who began his Krav Maga journey in June of 2011. He maintains a blog of his Krav Maga experiences, starting from his very first lesson, at kravmagajourney.com. In addition to the blog, he has an active presence on the *Krav Maga Journey* Facebook page. He currently lives in New England with his family and their two dogs.